BOULDERS ON THE RUNWAY

Thoughts on a lifetime of business experience

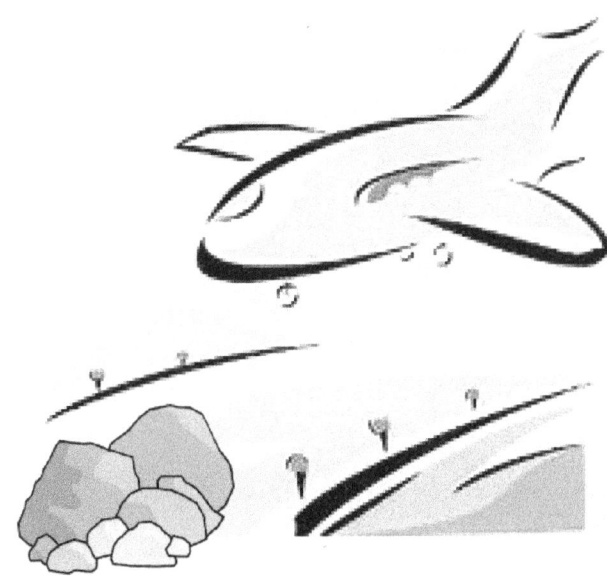

By Graham B King

Dedication

This book is dedicated to all those colleagues and friends that I have worked with throughout my career. Without you it would have been impossible to write this book as I have learnt so much from each one of you. I thank you for that and wish you all the best.

It is also dedicated to the most important people in my life.

Contents

INTRODUCTION

After working in various businesses for over 42 years I wanted to help you as a business professional to avoid the many pitfalls and stupidities that you are almost certain to come across in your day to day interactions. I hope that my experience will help you to be more effective as an individual and ultimately lead to better results for your organisation. No matter where you are in the world, in which ever organisation you are working in, you are almost certain to come across the situations described in this book. By being aware of them in advance you will be one step ahead of your teams and your colleagues. You must be smarter than they are so that you can drive them towards the rights solution(s) and get the results that you seek.

I have worked in various roles in lots of functions in several countries around the world and in many different sectors. The same things crop up again and again. I believe they are a function of human interactions in an organisation where the vast majority of people are generally poorly trained and operate in a sloppy and careless way, no matter how intelligent or well educated they perceive themselves to be.

I am currently a Senior Executive and International Company Director for a multi-national service company that operates in over 100 countries across the globe. It is exhausting to see the same errors, mistakes and so-called solutions touted as the way forward. Of course, many things must be considered by senior management to develop, grow and shape your organisation no matter what its purpose so I hope that by recognising, eliminating and or avoiding these situations you will be more effective and efficient than your colleagues.

Why Boulders on the Runway? Recently it has become trendy in business speak to refer to aircraft and airline analogies. A few weeks ago, after an 8-hour meeting a senior colleague stated that 'We were losing altitude' - in plain

English people were tired which was not surprising. I don't understand why in business people must use such stupid statements when it is perfectly simple to communicate what you want to say with clear and precise language. So, in today's trendy business speak 'Boulders on the Runway' is suitable analogy for what I want to get across. I have touched on many subjects lightly merely to highlight them. This short book is not intended to be an in-depth explanation or analysis of the topics under discussion but a light-hearted look at today's business world. I have also tried to inject some humour into my writing which I hope makes you at least smile every now and again!

THOUGHTS ON STRATEGY

Mission, Vision, Values

For most people understanding the definition of what mission, vision and values means is a challenge and then understanding all the bullet point lists that hang under each of them is even more daunting. You see these bullet points all the time - posters lining office walls, mouse mats and 3D origami card models on desks all proclaiming the way forward.

Then add the fact that all three (Mission, Vision and Value) are likely to change every couple of years as new people take the helm, ditch the old versions, bring in some consultants and invent some new bullet points – nice work if you can get it!

The whole process is ridiculously complicated, and most staff simply pay lip service, ignore them or joke about them when they can (which is probably a lot more than you imagine). If your organisation produces drainpipes, then that is what it does – it is not a mission – flying to the moon is a mission. A vision is what religious people experience and convinces them to follow a particular calling and, in my book, values are the monetary value of assets.

So, dump all of these and call a spade a spade. That is not to say that you should not articulate what your organisation does but just keep it simple.

Strategy

It is quite amazing how an organisation's strategy can change like the wind. When new people come along, they invariably reinvent the wheel which quite frankly simply serves to confuse the employees. How many times have you heard or read about your organisation's new strategy? One minute:

- Centralisation v decentralisation
- Going up market then down market
- Outsourcing, then insourcing
- Cost cutting then a spending spree
- Targeting new clients/customers/users and then focusing on existing clients/customers/users
- Geographical expansion, then retrenchment
- New products/services then reducing product/service range
- New sales channels then back to the old ones

- Vertical integration then horizontal integration then reversing it all.

It is never ending, and it is fascinating how everyone drinks to 'coolade' one day for one strategy, then different 'coolade' for the next strategy.

Six Questions

In my view strategy is very simple and you need to answer only six questions.

1. What is the dominant foundation of your organisation? There are only 3 answers:
   a. Low price and or cheap/value for money
   b. Innovative and creative
   c. Focused on your customers or clients.

Pick only one – the others are important, but they are not the dominant driving force.

2. Who are your customers or clients? There are billions of people in the world and no organisation can serve all of them, so you must make a choice and be very specific and clear about who to serve and focus on.
3. What products or services does your organisation provide?

4. What is your business model? Are you a manufacturer, a retailer, a service provider, a design house or wholesaler?
5. What is your geographic reach, stretch and or ambition?
6. Should you be involved in any other related businesses, services or products?

You then need to know where you are today which is where analysis comes into play – not paralysis by analysis but thoughtful analysis that provides you with some insight. All too often analysis becomes an end in itself and more and more analysis is undertaken which yields nothing new. Once you have your basic analysis you can then work out where you want to be and can develop and execute action plans to achieve your objectives.

Communicate Your Plans

One of the biggest failings with strategy and related action plans is the failure to communicate your plans to your staff. If you were running an orchestra your musicians would all be playing from the same musical score. Imagine what it would sound like if they didn't! In many organisations some people know the current strategy and act accordingly, others are working towards the old strategy and in some cases, may even be operating to a set of strategic plans several versions old. So, is it any wonder that organisational performance is sub-standard?

It is vital to communicate very clearly to each member of staff what the strategy is and how they can play their part. By this I don't mean giving them coffee mugs and pens with some anodyne statements printed on them. Think of it as handing musical scores to each employee. Plans should be detailed, specific and staff should believe what they are doing and why, otherwise they simply won't operate effectively. This will take a lot of energy and it is time consuming but as in the orchestra analogy without the correct score the performance will be dreadful.

Once you have developed your action plans and communicated them to everyone you can them monitor and track your performance over time and adjust your actions where appropriate. There is no need for a huge strategic planning department or for expensive teams of consultants. You and your team should be able to work this all out – if not get a new team.

THOUGHTS ON CLIENTS

Client Research

Most client research is a waste of time simply because people lie. They will nearly always tell you what you want to hear or what they think you want to hear rather than what they actually think or do. The best way to understand your customers or clients is to observe them. Watch what they do. It is far more insightful and revealing and will actually provide you with some valuable research. The best way to observe your clients or customers is to do so when they are unaware – then you will get powerful insights into what makes them tick and what choices they make.

Client Experience

Most organisations pay lip service to the client experience as very few organisations come anywhere close to providing a stress-free client experience. Just look at the Net Promoter Scores of many organisations. They will have business improvement programmes focused on the client, teams of staff to handle client complaints, call centres, client care centres, twitter feeds and Facebook pages. Yet still the client experience is appalling. These are some of the challenges that clients and customers face when attempting to deal with organisations:

- Trying to get through the myriad of menu options at call centres including dealing with automated voice technology
- Trying to get through on the phone to the right person to speak to
- Trying to get a refund
- Trying to exchange some goods

- Waiting on the phone with no idea where you are in the queue but being tortured by 'musak' and being told to go to the website to solve your issue
- Being asked for passwords, security words, account numbers time after time especially when being transferred around an organisation.
- Not being informed when something is delayed
- The inability to find out how to contact an organisation on a website (it is a deliberate policy in many organisations to avoid speaking to clients/customers).

All the new tools and communication methods now available have quite frankly in most cases made the client experience worse rather than better. You need to drill down into each transaction in detail and work through how to make them as smooth and as easy as possible from the client's point of view then train and train your staff. Then monitor your interactions with your clients and rather than adding more complaint staff to your teams get to the root cause of the complaints and sort that – much cheaper and better for everyone concerned.

If you ever want to complain about something get in contact with the Chairman of the organisation in question – never customer services or the helpline.

THOUGHTS ON PRODUCTS AND SERVICES

Services

Services are often poorly designed and properly thought through. Occasionally you come across an interaction with an organisation that works smoothly but that is the exception. With all the abundance of technology it is astounding that so many services are inadequate. What is needed is fresh thinking and challenging existing ways of doing things. It sounds sensible but it is very rare indeed.

Products

We live in a world with an amazing array of products at our fingertips – more than ever. Many of these are truly fantastic but one problem that does exist is how complex some are to use and understand. Sometimes even getting a product out of its packaging is a challenge. There just needs to be more attention paid to the ease of use and in particular to instructions which in some cases can be perplexing.

Cross Selling

In an organisation that sells products or services I believe that there is a natural level of cross selling – i.e. people buying related products or services. These should of course be marketed and promoted in a sensible and practical way. I have never yet seen any cross-selling campaign be successful. It is often tabled as the answer to falling sales, increasing revenues or a lost opportunity but it never delivers so minimise the level of resources that are applied to cross selling and focus instead on new products/ services or other expansion opportunities.

Business Process Service Development

So much time is spent by many people in re-inventing the wheel particularly when it comes to business process services or the approach to doing things. For example, how many times can you reinvent how to manage a project, how to approach analysis, how to manage change or how to reengineer processes. It is an industry in itself and each new approach is promoted as the answer.

IT people in particular are experts at inventing new ways to develop systems (of course with a whole new language to go with it – e.g. swim lanes, sprints, scrum master, story points).

At the end of the day most of the effort is wasted and could be used more effectively getting things done. If you are confronted with this nonsense, tell people what you think and get them to focus on getting the basics right.

THOUGHTS ON CHANGE

All Change is Good.

The Oxford English dictionary defines heresy as 'Opinion profoundly at odds with what is generally accepted'. Albeit that this originally applied to religion it is used today to ensure anyone that challenges change is akin to a heretic. I hear time and time again that all change is good - it isn't.

Change is good when it is well thought through, developed to resolve a particular problem, set of issues or to improve things. Change for change sake is destructive, expensive, stressful and pointless as more change will then be required to sort out the mess that is created. It takes a brave person indeed to challenge this current orthodoxy, in effect to be a heretic. I urge you to resist ill thought through change and to be assertive in the face of all those so-called professionals who will believe that change for change sake is what is required.

Don't be frightened of change

It is amusing to watch those TV programmes
that go back decade by decade and review the
changes that occurred within that decade and
how they compare with today. When you listen
to the music, see the fashions, cars, homes,
technologies, entertainments and realise how
far social values have changed you understand
how much change there has been within all our
lives. Much of it good, some maybe less so but
people generally don't like change when
confronted with it but if they didn't accept
change, they would still be in the past. So, keep
changes going all the time, small ones are best
and over time they accumulate and result in a
step change.

Evolution not Revolution

Revolutions are traumatic, disruptive, dangerous, costly and often leave a trail of destruction behind them. It is far better to take incremental steps to get to what you want to achieve as this breeds success, instils confidence and encourages people to keep moving ahead. People are inherently conservative and have powerful motives and drives to maintain the status quo – so gentle nudges are far more effective than major leaps.

So, when you are trying to implement change it doesn't work to lay out a bright new future. You need to start with what is wrong today and that there is something wrong with the status quo. When people acknowledge that the status quo isn't good enough anymore then they will be prepared to change but only step by step.

Don't Overcomplicate

It usually doesn't take very long for a smart person to work out and understand what an organisation does and how it works. I would hazard a guess and say if you are really focused you can get most of it worked out in a couple of weeks.

Middle managers will tell you how complicated everything is and how you can't possibly begin to understand what is going on without the need for years and years of experience. The reality is that they are the complicating factors and will do everything they can to maintain complexity. That is why they are middle managers because they can't see the bigger picture and never will. So, listen to them for a bit, then make up your mind and move on.

Any potential high flyers in the middle ranks will get it and see the big picture and you will be able to spot them from a mile away. They should be encouraged and promoted, the others will remain where they are continuing to complain and should probably be replaced in due course.

THOUGHTS ON PEOPLE

The Irritating Little F---.

There is always an irritating Little F--- in every organisation. They are the ones that comment on something but add no value whatsoever and are just plain irritating – like a little dog snapping at your heels. For example, when a corporate e-mail is sent out, they:

- Comment on grammar or punctuation
- Point out a spelling mistake
- Make some snide comment about policy or how it doesn't apply to them.

And of course, they reply to all staff just to make their point.

I see this over and over again when for example something serious is being discussed and the irritating Little F--- will stick their oar in just because they can – not that they are adding value or pointing out something important.

You need to neutralise these individuals or best of all get them out of your organisation all together.

Not everyone rises to the top

People are different and have different skills
and capabilities but there appears to be a
working assumption (again heresy to deny it)
that everyone must be promoted, must be
moving on in their career and reaching for the
stars. The problem is that this isn't going to
happen. Some people are very happy doing a
job and find fulfillment in their life in other ways
– work is just a means to an end. So, it is okay if
some people just want to do a job or are happy
to stay where they are.

Prima Donnas

All organisations have Prima Donnas – the people who think that they are critical to an organisation's success and that they are irreplaceable – newsflash – they aren't!

Prima Donnas are often tolerated but they also need to be kept in line. They do drive success and do contribute but they are often highly emotional, irrational, abusive, childish, self-centred and non-conformist. They need a firm hand and quite frankly must be treated like children, given firm guidelines and rules and told off when they step out of line.

All Prima Donnas can easily be replaced by the next ones waiting in the wings. You just need to look at the film world – there are always new actors and actresses coming up the ranks to challenge the current favourites. It is exactly the same in any organisation.

Consequences

In your organisation if there are consequences for not doing something or misbehaving don't let people get away with it. This is especially true of Prima Donnas. If people see others getting away with things it breeds resentment, a 'them and us' culture and a divisiveness that is very unhealthy for your organisation. Be cruel to be kind.

Survival of the Fittest

Charles Darwin was right – it is about the survival of the fittest aka smartest. There is a whole industry today that supports failure – it starts in school where no one must fail, and everybody has to be good at everything. It is simply impossible and it's cruel because people grow up thinking they capable and will get a huge shock when they join the real world and realise how tough it really is.

The failure industry continues to thrive in the workplace where it is almost impossible to call someone out for making a mistake or not being capable of doing something. People really should realise what they are good at and what they are not good at – not everyone has the same gifts.

I also blame TV talent shows with their judges' comments invariably stating that the contestant in front of them 'deserves it'. There is now a whole generation in the workplace that thinks and actually believes that they 'deserve it'.

Nothing is mentioned about hard work, building upon success, shaping character and establishing credibility

If you want to succeed you have to be smarter than the rest - fact. In today's society that must be done in a relatively polite way as brashness, over ambition and aggressiveness are not valued. So, you need to be clear about what you want, work out in your organisation how to get there then work to achieve your ambitions. If it doesn't work where you are then move on.

Snowflakes or Millennials

The generation of people who have grown up with current technology have a completely different perspective on the world than previous generations. They think differently and have a completely alternative view of the world and the importance of their place in it. They think they deserve everything and the concept of working step by step to achieve something is alien to them. They are fortunate to have been brought up in a very pleasant society with access to worldly goods and travel that was unheard of even 30 years ago. Whilst they are coming into organisations to work, they are going to have hard knocks as they come to realise how hard they will have to work to be successful.

Kill at Birth

Several animals kill their young at birth - the crocodile springs to mind. In organisations, there are many crocodiles lurking in the undergrowth ready to pounce and kill off any initiative that they don't like. It is quite extraordinary how many there are and how powerful they can be.

Even though everyone agreed to move ahead with an initiative, funding and resources were found, implementation plans were developed and communicated well then just as things are coming to life the 'crocodiles' emerge telling you that they never really supported this, never believed it would work and that we really should stop and move onto something else - usually their idea of course.

Selectivity

Clever people are very good at selectivity. They can selectively:

- Listen when they want
- Read what they want
- Understand if they need to
- Focus when it pleases them
- Ignore technology when they want to.

This is all well and good, but it means that they can walk away from responsibility as they pretend it is not their remit or beyond them. Just see how selective they can be when discussing their remuneration – suddenly their mathematical skills are Nobel prize winning. Plus, when they say they can't use a new computer system how come they can shop on line and book wonderful holidays on line at home?

Wired

People are genuinely wired differently, and, in many cases, the hard wiring can't be changed so don't bother. You can never expect a finance person to be creative or a marketing person to enjoy sticking to budgets. It just doesn't happen. So, the best thing to do is to just accept it as a fact and where appropriate complement individuals with other staff to balance out their hard wiring. When you come to know an individual's personality and think you can get them to change, attempting to get them to do so is virtually nigh on impossible so as above don't bother.

Entrepreneurs

These are rare individuals and should be cherished within your organisation. They will be creative, drive forward ideas and initiatives and will take risks. They are not afraid of failing but they are afraid of not trying so let them try. Sometimes it may not work out, but you don't know what will work until you try it.

Recruitment

There is so much talked about how to recruit, how to interview, what to look for in a candidate, how to read a CV and so on. There are a few things that you need to look for:

1. Initial impression – experts will tell you that you shouldn't make up your mind in the first 10 seconds but unfortunately that his how the mind works. When someone comes in for an interview you instantly make a judgement and usually it is correct.

2. Look for someone who is morale, good, stands up for the right things – then you know that you can trust them to do an excellent job in any situation.

3. People who have overcome obstacles are far more useful than those who have had a gilded existence. Overcoming obstacles shows that the individual can handle a

situation, work out what to do and come out the other side. They are not fazed by problems.

4. A global outlook is vital these days as the world is a small place and we increasingly all interact with each other across the globe. Travel broadens the mind which is a useful analogy and a global perspective and understanding will lead to better results.

5. Find the individuals to work for you who want to offer something to your organisation, not the ones that want to use your organisation to achieve their own objectives – after all you must be recruiting to solve a problem – so can the candidate?

Another point to remember is that if candidates are difficult coming into the organisation, questioning things, their package, their benefits etc. they will always be difficult and a bane in your life.

THOUGHTS ON CORPORATE DEPARTMENTS

IT

The amount of money and resources spent on IT systems is vast in almost all organisations, but it is usually the case that the systems do not do what they are supposed to do or only do half the job. I simply don't understand why in most organisations poor systems are tolerated. It is sheer laziness that results in systems that require lots of workarounds, manual interventions or situations in which key transactions aren't covered by system functionality.

Of course, there will be many staff employed in the IT department with additional consultants and off-site staff and programmers based in cheaper locations/countries. Despite all this resource and effort, the systems produced will still be defective and these resources will spend hours and hours telling you why things can't be improved or that things are impossible or that budgets are too limited.

So why does happen time and time again? The problem is that programmers end up programming bad requirements. Time and energy must go into designing business requirements down to the nth degree. This step is increasingly skimmed over and especially with the new approach to system build (agile) which is to build a skeleton system, try it out and refine it. This never works because some fundamental building block will have been put in place at the start or omitted and then it becomes too expensive or time consuming to reverse it, so you end up with a compromise. Compromise means you have less than optimal functionality and or the need to employ more staff than necessary to plug the gaps. It is astounding that many processes still involve up to 50% of manual work when they have been redesigned and systematised.

This situation only gets worse and worse as IT capabilities improve and expectations rise. You must be fierce in terms of ensuring a thorough set of requirements are defined for your organisation.

Additionally, there is also the tendency to ditch functionality in order to deliver a system on time (or usually late). You then end up with a less than adequate system and missing functionality that will never be added in – you will then have years of less than optimum performance and associated cost. So, don't allow your IT teams to do this - force them to complete what is needed.

Websites

Today and increasingly so an organisation's website is fundamental to the workings, effectiveness and success of any organisation. It is so integral to today's world that it must be owned, developed and managed by the most senior leaders in the organisation. The biggest mistake that is repeated time and time again is having the marketing department be responsible for your organisation's website.

I cannot tell you what a fundamental error this is.

If you were building a house, you would use the right professionals:

- An architect, quantity surveyor, builder, plumber, electrician and plasterer.

Finally, if you needed, you would employ an interior designer who would sort out the colours, interior materials, look and feel etc. There is no way you would use an interior designer to lay your foundations, sort out the drainage, wire your building or install your bathrooms.

Then why or why do so many organisations use the equivalent to an interior designer – marketing. Marketing people are incapable of building a website as they have no interest in process, structure or architecture even though they often pretend they do. That is why so many websites are not fit for purpose. Think of your website as being akin to your offices, warehouse, factory, showrooms or stores. They are critical to your organisation and are designed specifically for your purposes by professional staff.

So, ensure that you use your best people to develop the architecture and foundation of your website, that its design is robust and intimately connected to your processes and procedures. Then you can invite marketing to make your website look attractive. I know that marketing people will protest saying that they now use analytics to look at behaviour, but they never make the connection between behaviour of users and the core processes of the organisation. They are simply incapable.

The best examples I can think of that demonstrate what I mean are so called luxury or fashion websites. They are usually beyond useless. They are managed by marketing and brand experts, usually have irritating introductions, virtually no ability to engage in any transactions and no ability to contact the organisation.

Common Website Errors

1. The pop-up box asking you to complete a survey immediately as you enter the site (analytics will tell you everything you need to know without irritating your clients or customers).

2. The pop-up box asking if you want to chat/talk to someone – if you did you would make contact.

3. The inability to make contact with a person when you want support.

4. Poor response times when you send in a request by e-mail. You are never sure that someone is looking at your request.

5. Transactions that look like they are going smoothly then nothing happens - you hit a black hole then the user must re-engage with the organisation in question.

6. Little or no information about progress or status of a transaction or order. Again, the user hits a black hole.

7. Menus and hierarchy that don't make logical sense – these are often constructed from an internal perspective not a user's.

8. Click to go somewhere and you end up somewhere else or in a loop.

9. Try to reverse your menu choice and you can't.

10. Pop up ads that interrupt your transaction.

Human Resources

Good HR people are worth their weight in gold and make great partners. However, some of them amaze me because they don't actually like people at all and treat them with disdain. They think of people as commodities and can be very cynical and unsympathetic – they are in the wrong job!

Legal

Lawyers are bright and well-educated people but usually in an organisation they are incapable of making a decision. They will give you lots of advice, opinions, what ifs, alternative scenarios and consequences but never 'pick a lane' as God forbid, they might have to defend their decision.

What can also tip you over the edge is when you ask for advice or a decision the response is frequently that we need to ask outside counsel which of course will cost you and arm and a leg.

As a senior leader, all you can do is to listen to their advice, ask them to leave the room and then make your own decision.

Finance

Finance people are like tradespeople. They have a particular skill and are there to do a specific job. They manage the flow of money, count it correctly, account for it accurately and ensure that the finances of your organisation are legal and compliant with whatever regulations and laws apply to your organisation. They can also be useful when seeking out funding for your organisation.

They do not and should not make business or commercial decisions. They can advise you of the impact and consequences of doing one thing or the other but that is it. Finance people are black and white and do not see shades of grey. Their brains are wired in such a way that they can't cope with ambiguity or uncertainty and they definitely have no flair or creativity. They are bad at making business decisions and shouldn't be encouraged or allowed to do so.

Understanding Finances

It is quite extraordinary how many people, and senior ones at that, do not understand even the most basics of how the finances of their organisation work. Whether it is producing revenues and income or managing to a cost budget the level of ignorance about the impact of actions on costs and revenue is beyond belief. It is essential that you ensure all your staff know how a profit and loss account works, how to read a balance sheet and what the consequences of their actions are.

Press

Journalists are some of the laziest people going.
They want to be spoon fed a story which is
usually done by your press department and
then printed word for word in whichever media.
The one thing that really winds me up are
journalists who attempt to invent a story
thinking they are clever and can spot something
that no one else has thought of. They always
see a conspiracy, a cover up, a strategic
mistake. They really are overrated and have an
inflated sense of their own importance.

Marketing and Logos

It is a law of nature that all marketing executives have to change the logo (or wordmark as they like to call it) when they arrive in a new organisation. They do so because most of them don't hang around very long and therefore need to leave some evidence that they were there – just like slugs that leave a trail in the morning – they are nowhere to be seen but you certainly know they were there.

This will cost the organisation a small fortune, require old materials with the old logo to be dumped and replaced with shiny new letter headings, business cards and the like. At some point the money will run out and usually the extremities of your organisation will never get the new logo, or it can't be changed in your IT system. Wait for the next new logo and you are more than likely to end up with an organisation with multiple logos dating from the reigns of previous marketing executives.

Digital Marketing

Digital marketing is clearly here to stay, and, in some cases, it is very powerful. However, there are instances where it adds no value at all and just creates activity, kudos for the marketing department and their statistics and entertainment for potential clients and customers. There are even new words that have been invented – edutainment and infotainment. You need to challenge the value of digital marketing and be tough and firm to ensure that you are getting the right results and not just creating a fan base of people who have no intention of engaging with your organisation.

Sponsorship

This appears to be a great solution to get your organisation's name out into the big wide world which will result in new business and new customers. I really doubt this. How many football supporters go home after watching a match and switch their bank accounts? Exactly. I think that if your organisation can receive inward sponsorship that is a good thing but if your organisation pays outward sponsorship, I really think it is a waste of money that could be spent in more effective ways.

THOUGHTS ON MEETINGS

Agendas

Agendas are obviously the standard way to take a meeting through a series of topics and issues to be dealt with. However, as more and more people have the attention span of a nat (all reinforced by the use of technology, twitter and text speak) it is increasingly difficult to keep people focused on the topic in hand as they stray off randomly and introduce unrelated topics that can easily descend into chaos. Then more and more people check out of the meeting and check their e-mails or even worse start their own side meetings. The only way to deal with this is to be forceful, stick to the agenda and lay the law down to the lawless.

Fantasising

Most people, most of the time are not focused in meetings – whether they are face to face, conference calls, skype calls or video/telepresence. They spend 80/90% of the time fantasising or day dreaming and the more people in a meeting the better as the probability that you will actually have to do something or say something is reduced – hence more time to fantasise!

Conference calls are great as you can pretend you are listening intensively whilst thinking about something else. For video and telepresence meeting you can always sit out of range - you are in the meeting doing your job, but no one can see you!

It always amazes me how meetings are always set up in units of 30 minutes and more often 60 minutes – that means there is plenty of time for day dreaming. So, in a one-hour meeting 80% of fantasy time equals 48 minutes – far better than having to do any real work!

So, try this:

- Set up a meeting for 15 minutes or better still 12 minutes – that will shock!
- Hold a face to face meeting in a room/space with no chairs – that meeting won't last very long!
- Randomly ask questions or elicit comments from attendees – to disrupt their day dreaming!
- Don't let people sit behind you.

Mobile Devices

In a typical meeting today, everybody brings along at least one mobile device (if not two), then spends most of the time, before, during and after the meeting, checking their e-mails, not taking calls (as that might appear a bit to rude) or surfing the internet. If you ask them a question or ask them to contribute you are interrupting them as they have far more important things to do than be in the meeting in the first place.

So perhaps disinvite them to the meeting next time and make an important decision without them.

At the next meeting instruct them to place all devices on silent and put them away out of sight.

THOUGHTS ON TRAINING

Training

When I was sixteen, I started to work as a waiter to save up for driving lessons and thankfully I was trained how to be a proper waiter. For example, when serving food, you serve the plate to the left of the customer and clear from the right. The reason for this is that both the waiter and the customer know what is happening, what to expect and how to interact with each other silently. Get it wrong and the customer may move slightly to one side or the other and hit the plate, spilling food on the table.

A very simple example but one that highlights the importance of training people to do things properly. You need to ensure that your staff are trained to do things correctly and properly.

Management Training

The concept of management training is no different today than it was, in say, Roman times. Management is simply getting things done through other people and people haven't changed for thousands of years let alone since the Roman empire. Why then is management training reinvented time and time again? The reason is that management training is an industry that keeps itself alive by pretending to reinvent something new. The basics of management are eternal and don't change over time. Things are less brutal than in Roman times and social mores are different than in historical times, but effective management is still the same.

I can honestly say I don't think that I have ever learnt anything on a management course that I use day to day. Spending a day or several days with others, usually in some nice places simply has not worked

The best way to learn about management is to:

1. Study and understand basic psychology and management theories.
2. Watch and learn from effective colleagues around you especially as you are starting in your career.

The three most important things that I ever learnt were:

1. Use Mind Maps to think through any problem, presentation or topic you have to work on
2. As a senior executive spend at least 10% of your time at work planning and thinking about the future. If you don't do this – who will?
3. Be nice to people, explain what you want them to do and why, give them freedom to get on with the job then either monitor progress or check in when a task or job is complete.

Management Gurus

Management gurus are an industry that is self-perpetuating and rarely if at all have ever been involved in any real management, position of responsibility or having to make serious decisions. There is nothing worse than a fully-fledged academic spouting forth theories and advice when they have no real-life organisational experience. Most news programmes with business segments are full of these sorts of people today as they try to fill their 24hour service.

Anyone who teaches management practice should have had at least 10 years' senior practical management experience before being let loose on educating young minds or aspiring managers.

A Week in the Hills

It seems to me that there are lots of so-called management development courses that require you to spend a week walking in the Welsh hills, the Lake or Peak district or if you lucky a nice hot Mediterranean country. To say that these are leadership or management development courses is a disservice – they are adventure holidays paid for by your organisation and given to employees to keep them motivated and on-side. Good for you if you can get on one of these or even better if you run the company offering these. Just don't think that they will have any lasting impact at all apart from lots of photos on your mobile phone.

The Conference or Retreat

Like a week walking in the Welsh hills the conference or retreat is another form of holiday. They are always held in nice locations, in 4- or 5-star hotels or facilities and are a welcome break from the day to day routine. You get to meet old colleagues, chat to new ones, have some pleasant food and probably more alcoholic drink than you should. Evenings in the bar always go on far too late and nocturnal activities usually follow for those who are not used to staying away from home – it is all too exciting!

The Workshop

At a conference or retreat there will usually be plenty of workshops where grown adults get to behave like children again – sulking, dominating, shouting, bullying and the like. I detest workshops. They are the most infantile way of getting things done and always result in the unreadable flip chart at the end with 3 recommendations, top 10 to do's or 5 best brain-stormed ideas that everyone supposedly agrees on. There is always the 3-minute presentation of the results by one workshop member bullied into doing it. Finish the presentations, bin the flip charts (or hand to a junior go-fer to type up the unreadable) then off for another drink and night in the bar followed by more nocturnal goings on. Plus, at the end of the day in the vast majority of cases nothing will result from the workshops.

THOUGHTS ON PRESENTATIONS

Death by PowerPoint

My mother used to be a teacher and in the 1970's and 80's she was always producing what she called 'visual aids'. These were often large pieces of card with images and drawings on them to convey what the topic in question was and were very useful.

Then comes along the person who invented PowerPoint and whilst it is a useful software package it has created a whole wave of crimes.

Powerpoint Crimes

1. I, the presenter am clever and you audience member are stupid, so I will read out the words on my slides – one by one.
2. I, the presenter am very clever and you audience member are very stupid, so I will use my extended car radio aerial or hi-tech red pointer and I will tap/highlight each word as I read them out one by one.

3. I, the presenter know so much about my topic that I have put everything I know on one slide, so you can't possibly see it.
4. I, the presenter know so much about my topic that I have 100 slides to present to you.
5. I, the presenter have used lots of on-line stock photography (that you will have seen a million times before).
6. Presenters use phrases like 'I'll come back to that later' or 'I'll deal with that later in the presentation' – most people's heart sinks at that prospect.
7. Most people can recall nothing about most presentations they see or hear – perhaps the first couple of minutes then they refocus when they hear 'and in conclusion' so potentially the last couple of minutes as well. The rest is a haze. Why? Because people settle, they are comfortable, can fantasise, they are passive. That is because slides /or the deck is boring, telling you what you already know, establishing

credibility/track record and how wonderful the organisation or product/service. The problem is that the audience doesn't care about any of this.

How to give a good presentation

- Be original
- Look enthusiastic
- Use only a few slides or even better revert to drawing an original drawing (keep it simple) on a white board or flip chart – people remember this format far more effectively and remember drawings – no one ever recalled a list of bullet points.
- Don't state the obvious – who you are, who your audience are
- State the problem and rock the audience's mental status quo – people don't act until they must.
- Disturb them, scare them a little then offer them a way forward – a path to a brighter safer future a new status quo.
- Be remarkable, be memorable. Try it – it really works, and people will remember you....

THOUGHTS ON PERSONAL PERFORMANCE

E-mail

E-mail has been a tremendous invention that has truly revolutionised communications and how things are done. It is however at the point of getting out of control and becoming a hindrance to effective operation. The following are examples of such hindrances:

- Typing in red text and or capital letters – this means shouting and anyone who sends me an e-mail like this results in the delete key being used. It is not acceptable.

- Sending an e-mail to lots of people with no idea who is to respond. What then happens some recipients may respond and exclude or include others until you have total chaos.

- Selective facts – in the days of writing a memo it had to be thoughtful, well laid out and argued as it was usually the only document on that topic. What happens now is information is selective and when the e-mails start being answered and forwarded the facts loose out and you end up with e-mail ping pong and virtually no idea what is going on. No doubt you have printed out an e-mail chain which was probably, 20, 30, 40 or more pages long.

- Implementation by e-mail – it is common to hear someone say that something has been done because an e-mail has been sent. This is especially critical when it comes to implementation – you cannot implement by e-mail and I cannot stress that enough. Recipients may not read the e-mail, may delete it and because e-mail is so easy it is not taken seriously enough. If you want to implement something you must talk to people.

- Attempting to make major decisions by e-mail. It is a common and huge mistake for serious and major decisions to be discussed via e-mail with a group of people who often respond with one-liners that move the discussion around like a slalom race but don't get to the heart of the matter. You need to be brave enough to stop the e-mail banter and get some serious face to face time with a well thought out document to guide the conversation and decision-making process.

- Unsolicited and junk e-mail - this is a growing industry and menace as you can receive hundreds of these every day. Finally junk mail in the post is declining substantially but the rise of e-mail junk is far worse, expanding and can be threatening. I urge you to use the block menu to stop these irritating and time-consuming distractions.

Word and Excel Crimes

Both of these software packages are fantastic and really have brought about great benefits for all sorts of reasons. But again, crimes are committed:

Word Crimes

1. People who put tables of numbers in a word document that aren't embedded excel mean you can't check them to see if the totals are correct for example or change them.
2. Using too much formatting that makes a document impossible to manage, control and finalise as the fonts, indents, headings and underlines change at will.
3. Sending round 'marked up' documents that become impossible to read as more mark ups are added. Legal people love doing this.

Excel Crimes

1. Merged cells – the biggest crime of all as you can't then manipulate a spreadsheet and its value is significantly reduced.
2. Hiding columns so you cannot see how figures are derived.
3. Not using 0 for the start of axes on graphs – it always gives a misleading impression.
4. Failing to present data is a way that it can be manipulated or sorted.

Holidays

A holiday is defined as: 'A time when someone does not go to work or school but is free to do whatever they want such as travel or relax'.

All seems to make perfect sense apart from the fact that the concept of a holiday has changed to basically mean one where you end up working but from somewhere else. People don't respect holidays anymore. Before the advent of the mobile phone and being on line permanently people simply couldn't get hold of you. Now it is a complete nightmare where colleagues expect you to deal with e-mails in real time, answer calls, be on conference calls, read documents and simply do your normal work. It drives me insane when someone sends you an e-mail starting:

- Sorry to bother you on holiday but…………
- I know you are away on holiday but……….

I was advised by an English Lord that if your team can't cope when you are on holiday – get another team. Perfect advice for today's world. Go on holiday and only allow yourself to be contacted in a dire emergency.

Multi-tasking

As with 'all change is good' it is also the case that 'multi-tasking is also good' and again heresy to suggest otherwise. Well let me tell you – multi-tasking is not good, it is not effective and results in poor results. People seem to want to wear multi-tasking as a badge today to prove how effective they are. Well if they concentrated on getting one thing done at a time and doing it properly, they would be more effective. Multi-tasking is like a butterfly fluttering around and if your staff believe in it you should firmly disavow them of this ridiculous notion.

Stress

Stress is good and an essential part of life. It is exciting, keeps one stimulated and adds to the spice of life. Too much stress is truly awful and damages your life, your mind and your physical body.

Why in most organisations are people subjected to levels of stress that are intolerable? You just have to look around you at work. If animals were stressed to that degree can you imagine the uproar? I think a lot more attention needs to be paid to the levels of stress at work and that it should be thought about and talked about far more than it is. As the world has become more exciting and possibilities abound for many people that didn't exist even a generation ago care is needed to avoid burn out or people living a sub-optimal life.

Olympics

If senior executives were in the Olympics such as a sprinter or top athlete, they would be surrounded by a whole team of people dedicated to their wellbeing and success. For example, it is not unknown for an athlete to have:

- A nutritionist
- A coach in their respective field
- A masseur
- A doctor
- A physiotherapist
- A psychologist
- An alternative medical practitioner.

Now when it comes to a senior executive, they might have access to one or two of the above but never the whole package. Business people today are expected to:

- Not require the normal number of hours of sleep to remain alert

- Travel around the globe and land feeling refreshed (have you seen how the airline adverts portray this - most unlike the reality of feeling like sh—when getting off an overnight flight – even if you flew in business class)
- Take sleeping tablets when travelling (that makes people super grumpy)
- Skip breakfast and/or eat rubbish for lunch and/or dinner
- Live on coffee and copious amounts of alcohol
- Work excessively long hours in stressful situations which results in both physical and mental problems
- To have breakfast meetings, lunches, dinners, drinks.
- Tolerate low level illness.
- Commute in conditions that we wouldn't tolerate for animals.

So, as you are probably not an Olympic athlete or have access to the support network list above you need to create your own Olympic programme so that you can operate as effectively as a Gold Medal winner. Take control of your time, your physical and mental wellbeing and develop a regime and programme that works for you.

Dashboards

A dashboard is essential when you are driving a car or flying a plane. It tells you at a glance what is going on and helps the driver/pilot to make informed decisions. I drive an electric car and the dashboard is quite complex with many symbols in assorted colours that requires a reference manual (on-line) to work out what is going on. Well at least it is only one dashboard.

In an organisation, the concept of the dashboard makes sense, just as it does when driving a car. However, the problem is the number of dashboards – it is like driving 30+ cars at once. Dashboards seem to breed and now there are so many it is impossible to use them. Every new initiative requires a dashboard, every new project requires a dashboard and every department produces a dashboard – each of them totally different in concept, design and value. I even have a complete set of dashboards that I must interrogate – totally the opposite of the concept of a dashboard.

As well as dashboards, there are many reports, financial statements and ad hoc reports that are produced. The industry of management reporting and business intelligence has got completely out of control and each year brings a new software release and a wave of new dashboards and reports.

You need a magic gun that destroys all management reports and dashboards, so you can start again and control everything that is produced so that information flowing around the organisation is consistent and can be read and understood by everyone. It's a tough ask but one that is absolutely necessary.

Along with the proliferation of dashboards is the proliferation of Key Performance Indicators. The operative word here is KEY not indicator. Once again, the management information industry generates as many indicators as possible (because they have to fill all their dashboards). What a senior person needs are the KEY indicators on ONE dashboard. If you select the right key indicators any organisation can be managed and directed from one A4 piece of paper (or iPad screen). You just have to get the indicators right to tell what is going on and more importantly what is going wrong.

Machine Gun

A typical day at work in 2019 often feels as though you are being sprayed with bullets from a machine gun. Subjects, topics and issues come at you so quickly and so frequently that it is almost impossible for your brain to cope. With the added complexity of mobile phones, landlines, iPads, PCs or laptops, e-mails, people, conference calls, video calls it is a wonder anyone survives a typical day.

This is when you have to put up a defence mechanism to deflect the bullets so that you can take control. I blame all of this on technology and the irrational expectations of people that they can expect answers or responses in real time. It simply can't happen and is quite frankly bad for everyone.

You must control technology. How?

1. Only read e-mails during working hours

2. Rarely respond to an e-mail in real time, otherwise people will expect it all the time
3. Don't allow people to interrupt you in your office - almost impossible with the proliferation of 'open plan' offices but let people know that you are not to be disturbed
4. Don't sign documents when other people want – make them put them in a queue – they will hate it - but you have control
5. Switch off PCs, phones and iPads for a period every day or leave them aside for a bit – they literally fry your brain waves.

Happiness

If you are unhappy it is your fault. If you are in a situation which makes you unhappy get out of it. No-one is forcing you to do anything against your will and you alone are responsible for your happiness. People blame everything and everybody apart from themselves. They are victims; they had an unhappy marriage, faltering career, deprived childhood or whatever. Overcoming setbacks and obstacles is a true test of character and only you can reach inside yourself to find happiness. There is so much help available these days it is terrifying – just find a book or look online then work through whatever issues you have and get yourself into a good place.

How to be more effective and successful

- Watch successful people and how they operate – then apply what you find useful to your daily life
- Live in a nice area
- If you drive, drive a nice car
- Wear nice clothes
- Be well groomed
- Take a multi-vitamin and mineral every day along with a cod liver oil capsule – will keep you in good working order
- Eat healthy food – best approach is to buy ingredients and make meals yourself – then you know what you are eating. God knows what food factories do to food as it rarely tastes lip smacking good. Plan your menus one week ahead, buy the food and enjoy preparing it. It is relaxing and will do you good.
- Get regular health checks so if anything is developing it can be nipped in the bud or managed.

- Always wear clean clothes, clean shoes and have a clean nose (literally of course) but I also mean no whiff of scandal about you or suspicion – be totally trustworthy
- Get the basics in life right first – the rocks in your life e.g. personal life, home, family life, working life, finances, financial protection, pensions, insurances, cars, – then the things that make life easier - the luxuries in life. You can't do it the other way around. It is like filling a tall vase with water first – you can't add rocks or sand. Add rocks first, sand and then you can fill it up with water.
- Be nice to people and show real empathy at those moments when it is really required and offer genuine help.
- Don't avoid talking about taboo subjects when they crop up. If someone has died recently those closest will just want to talk about that person – not about the weather.
- Give gifts at special moments. They will be remembered and treasured.

- Have fun, have a good sense of humour –
  don't be cheap, rude, vulgar or offensive.

It really is lonely at the top

It is an old saying but it is true. The more successful you are the less likely you are to make new friends at work. You hopefully made friends in your youth and early career and they always stay with you but when people look at you as a stepping stone to their own success what appears as friendship is nothing of the sort. People appear friendly enough but deep down they are using you to get ahead and when they no longer need you either because they move on or you do it is highly likely you will never hear from them again. Sad but true. Facebook and LinkedIn do help to make this a less traumatic event but over time I suspect clicks, likes and so on will fade away. It is well documented that most people only ever have 5 true friends. Count yours and look after them.

IN CONCLUSION

And finally

No-one on their deathbed ever said they wished they had worked more or stayed in the office later each night. Work must and should be put into perspective. Work is a means to an end and whilst it can be fulfilling there are far more important things in the world. What would you wish for on your deathbed? Whatever it is don't leave it too late, make it happen, enjoy life, live your dream and never regret……………..